Masks

Masks

poems by

Ruthann Robson

with an introduction by
Marge Piercy

The Leapfrog Press
Wellfleet, Massachusetts

Grateful acknowledgement is made to the editors and publishers of the following periodicals, journals and anthologies in which these poems, or versions of these poems, have appeared: Calyx: "each winter." Conditions: "Self-Portrait of Frida Kahlo Without a Moustache." Common Lives/Lesbian Lives: "chain-links." Florida Review: "neolithic [masks]," "the freeing of the hands." IKON: "Witchcraft in the Nuclear Ages," "waves, night." Kalliope: "the last decade of patriarchy." Labyrs: "not for my mother & father." New Letters: "Kathe Kollwitz, Graphic Artist, Sketches a German Working Class Woman," "Mary Cassatt, After Destroying the Letters of Edgar Degas," "The Animus of Diane Arbus, Photographer." Nimrod: "white and black photography." OUT/LOOK: "text." Trivia: "nightshade," "historicity," "authenticity." EARLY RIPENING: AMERICAN WOMEN'S POETRY NOW: "the consort," "Regine's Rebuke to Kierkegaard." LABOUR OF LOVE: "the fifth month." SPEAKING FOR OURSELVES: WOMEN OF THE SOUTH:"genealogy."

ISBN 0-9654578-5-0

Library of Congress Cataloging-in-Publication Data
Robson, Ruthann, 1956 -
    Masks : poems / by Ruthann Robson, with an introduction by Marge Piercy.
        p. cm.
    ISBN 0-9654578-5-0 (pbk.)
     1. Lesbians—Poetry. 2. Women—Poetry. I. Title.
PS3568.03187M3 1999
811'.54—dc21   98-25138
                                   CIP

Book design and typography by Erica L. Schultz.

Printed in the United States of America
10 9 8 7 6 5 4 3 2 1

Published by The Leapfrog Press
P.O. Box 1495, Wellfleet, MA 02667-1495, USA

Distributed in the United States by
Consortium Book Sales and Distribution
St. Paul, Minnesota 55114
(612) 221-9035 / (800) 283-3572

Contents

PART THREE
LIVING MY LIFE AS IF—

PART FOUR
THE DISTANCE BETWEEN OUR LOVE OF MASKS AND OUR LOVE

Introduction

Ruthann Robson's poems are about as sentimental as a rock dropped on the head. Her love poems are sensual, intelligent and fully operational. She never coddles herself. She is capable of great tenderness and also great precision. Her eyes are always wide open and so is her mind.

Her sense of humor is wicked and veiled, a function of her intelligence—wit in the old sense. She is aware of the shortcomings of language, the limits and the necessity of the political, the politics and the futility of labeling, the complexity of attempting to tell what ever we decide at the moment is the truth of our lives, present and past. Yet such intellectual subtlety never leads her to airiness or abstract palaver. Reality is always with her like her bones, and these poems, like fish, are full of bones. She is deeply concerned with the poetic resources of our language but never flowery or long-winded or pumped up with the flow. Rather, she etches. She writes with a very focused consciousness of what she is doing and trying to do.

I first met Ruthann Robson in the very early eighties. I was teaching at a writers' conference in Nashville, Tennessee, and she was in my class. She was associated with *Kalliope*—the excellent women's literary magazine still published today. Ruthann was by far the best poet in the class, and perhaps of any class I've taught since.

After the workshop, we stayed in touch and shared our work. Over the years. I have enjoyed and admired her fiction. I was surprised that she never had a book of her poetry published. It gives me a lot of pleasure and satisfaction to introduce her poems to you.

The combination of lawyer, academician and writer, working-class kid and lesbian mother is an interesting mix and the results are quite different than the male lawyers who write. She is often concerned with the law, but not particularly with legal procedure. The nuts and bolts of the law figure in her work, but rather as backgrounding than as the subject. Even when the case she is dealing with is on the sensational side, her treatment of it is never sensational. There is a dryness to her mental processes that enables her to deal with issues that would be lurid in other hands. Instead such material becomes insightful, witty or moving, and ultimately illuminating of the larger human condition. Consider the affecting and sometimes terrifying poem about the sixteen-year-old girl chained to a radiator by her mother, to keep her from the streets—the kind of story you might read in a tabloid while standing in the supermarket checkout line, but here rendered unforgettable and emblematic.

Her writing is powerfully centered in the female experience, but with a take that is different from any other writer I can think of. Her poetry is often passionate, but bathed in a clear hard light, even when she is dealing with the violent and the ultimately irrational. For someone who has such a demanding other career and a son to raise, her output is amazing. She is incredibly disciplined, as committed and intelligent a writer as I have ever known.

Some of these poems zero in on moments or trends in her own life, but she also examines the female experience through women in or associated with the arts as diverse as Frieda Kahlo, Alice B. Toklas, Diane Arbus, Käthe Kollwitz, Mary Cassatt, among others. She enters each of their lives sympathetically and speaks for them in a compassionate and persuasive voice. She is equally concerned with how they found or did not find love and with how these women worked and tried to preserve themselves and other women and that work.

Some of the poems are elliptical, oblique. They work through image and suggestion. They turn now one facet, now another into your gaze. The whole comes together in your mind. Other poems are as direct as a blow or a kiss. She works equally well in a short line and a long line. Some poems are imagistic, others, conversational.

I think you will enjoy experiencing a fine mind, a passionate and thoroughly political woman, here, in her poetry. You will meet many women in this book, mothers, daughters, lovers, women whom you will like and women who may frighten you or even anger you. They are all rendered with insight and clarity. They all people the world we live in or the past that has produced us. They are, if you like, also masks *of* and *for* women.

— Marge Piercy
Wellfleet, Massachusetts
1998

Masks

Genealogy

Almost better to be an orphan

than to be a woman holding sea-rotted
twigs and looking for ancestors;
clutching a driftwood divining rod that
will never discover a grand matriarch or
patron of the arts. My mothers had to work.

I come from a family of women with double
first names and dubious
surnames, of half sisters with half-told
stories, of women who would use their family
trees when firewood is scarce.

We have no leather bibles to edify
our descendants. In fact, the custom
among us has been to burn birth
certificates, to change names like
clothes stolen from someone else,

to hide from husbands and bad debts.
We moved across oceans and mountains and
never learned how to write a letter home.
You could say I have no history.
Of course, I could send twenty dollars

somewhere for a picture of my family
crest, complete with instructions in genealogy.
The rich spent years writing history
and now they need the cash. But what
could they tell me? But what would I find?

A white woman caring for her daughter dying
of childbed fever, and a hillbilly quilting
while coughing with black lung, and a chinese
woman ironing white boys' shorts, and a black
woman rolling other women's hair on Saturdays

and cigars during the week, and a woman not speaking
the language while she sewed in the cold
garment factory. A woman waitressing in Birmingham
and whoring in New Orleans and imprisoned
in Sydney. A blind woman selling newspapers and

a woman with one leg who wanted to love other women
but was afraid and a woman whose family changed
their names in disgrace and moved away, looking
for work where no one knew their debts and crimes.

These women are the salt
of my sea, the sweat that collects
on the rims of my scars. I do not need
to know their names, their places
of birth, their dates of death,

to know I am their daughter.

Part One

all the rest is myth

neolithic

1. *the wander*

there was a one-eyed animal at the water:
a snake
or a crane
a glint of fish or a goddess
i thought it was you

my lover
the same striated triangle
for a brow
the same length of incision
instead of a kiss

a laugh like a trick
we had played many games
when i was younger
the toads began to croak
their promises

i was held without arms
i could smell your bones
i could taste foam
i could hear the footsteps
of your heart

until the shadows opened
and the river hushed
until i could see a profile
that jutted unlike yours
under the slipping mask

but i was not sure
i spoke
i kept silent
i tried to see through my eyes
i let my fingers make decisions

until i could not remember
what you had told me about others
and why you had told me
until the words of anyone
no longer mattered

i wandered in the darknesses
guided by a thousand hands
what i saw was nothing
what i felt was everything
until the first lights slanted

and i was alone
the red chevrons on my breasts
were smeared with saliva
the alabaster buttons
of my hip-belt broken

i walked back
along the birch creek path
untangling my hair
with budded branches
my mask a face

2. *the wall*

the rains come
insisting
that green leaves float
from the trees swelling sure
as my belly

you spend your days modelling
mask after mask
mouthless masks
beaked masks
with angles sharp as lightning

a mask with eyelashes like snakes
a mask cropped with antlers
of encrusted feather
a mask with horns for ears
a mask with braids like mine

you ask
"is this the one?"
"is this?"
"more like this one?"
"less like that?"

you hang the masks on the wall
you make them watch
as you stroke me
hard one way
soft the next

you ask
"like this?"
"like that?"
"softer?"
"harder?"

the days are dark
with rain
more and more rain
when you let me sleep
i do not dream

i grow weary
i grow
i grow a sleek hair
from my breast
you pluck it out

wrapping it like thunder
on the apex
of the whitest mask
you kiss the O
of the mouthless stone

when white water spurts
from my lonely nipple
you drink it
you cry
you suck me dry

3. the wheat

dead birds
rise from the bed
of the bloated
swift river
their beaks rotting

small snakes
slide across my feet
circling my ankles
inching to my thighs
drawn by the heat

it is good to wander
the damp land
beyond all walls
the mist is like smoke
from my mother's breath

when the sky is wide
there are no secrets
i am welcome
by the bearded wheat
we are fertile

the women surround
ourselves
with our voices
we sing
the rain   the wheat   the woman

we put on and take off
each other's masks
we dance
we paint our faces
with the reddest ocher

one woman squats
she bleeds into the black
we clap
we sing
the blood   the wheat   the woman

the woman   the woman
with a ground full of giving
the woman   the snake
the crane   the glint
of fish   the goddess

white water leaks
from the clouds
of my breasts
a woman rubs it
on my stretching stomach

she rubs it on the wheat
it is good luck
we are good luck
we slit open a pig
in our own honor

4. *the whispers*

sometimes i eat flesh
i laugh
i smell poppies
i crack the corner of my mask
sometimes i listen

i like to listen
to the older women
they tell tales of whelks
found on the banks
of a green shining river

they speak words i can see
the sickle moon
the straight rain
the mating of leopard and bear
of women and masks

what the younger women say
they say in whispers
they say what you say
they say what they have heard
the men say

they say words without a shape
they say "father"
they say words they do not mean
they say "seed"
they shake their heads

when they say these things
still they say them
still they say what you say
they say women should not wander
they say women should not

they say women must wear masks
they say women must
they say that the wheat will grow
without me
they say i grow for men

the older women laugh
and sing louder
still the younger women whisper
still i cannot see their words
i listen

they say the toad song
does not grow a baby
they say it is the stick
of a man
of any man

they say what you say
that a mask
that a one-eyed animal
that a glint of fish or a goddess
means something

5. *the winter*

inside the walls
you keep it warm
you tend the fire
you feed the altar
you never take off the mask of hope

the women sing
the older women are loud
you shut them out
i can still see their words
clear as shadows

you model birthing masks for me
a twisting snake
a pair of cranes
a feeding fish
the faces of the goddesses you see

you are working
i am wary
a red welt rises
on my neck
from the slip of your hand

the water breaks
i know it is time
this is my night
i choose a mother's mask
the one like a pig

the women come for me
the women let me wail
i squat
i bleed into the black
they clap

i tear
i can smell bones
i can taste foam
i can hear footsteps
of two hearts

the child is alive
it is held to my breast
it sucks like the winter river
i stop bleeding
slowly slowly

i see the child
has one eye
like a kiss on its forehead
i see the child
its mouth an unbuttoned O

i see your words
your masks
i see the whispers
the women
i wrap all my arms around my child

6. *the warring*

you
you who said love
you
you who i let
winnow my wheat

you who let me sleep
while you took my child
my one-eyed beauty
to the winter river
green and freezing

you who weighted my baby
with mask after mask
mouthless masks
beaked masks
with angles sharp as lightning

a mask with eyelashes like snakes
a mask topped with antlers
of encrusted feathers
a mask with horns for ears
a mask with braids like mine

you who say words without a color
you who says "stranger"
you who say words you cannot mean
you who say "property"
you who try to hide your smile

you say the world
will start again
you say i must never wander again
you say i must never tell
you say i must

you clean the wall
you say soon it will be spring
you wash my face
you say there will be another baby
you say you know the secret

you say you promise
you say you know
i keep silent
you are stupid as the sun
i wait

i close my eyes
until i can see the shadows
of women singing
the older women
and the younger women

how could you not know
i am one of the women?
how could i not hold
your foot
as they rip out your beating heart?

7. *the water*

i wander the river
the green shining river
looking for whelks
looking for leopards
seeing the water

i wander near the edge
of the wheat
i wander near animals mating
the river is my only wall
i wander near the women

i listen
but not when they whisper women
should not
but not when they whisper women
must

i listen to the toad song
i wonder
winters come and go
i no longer bleed
i keep secrets

i wear a hip belt
it has alabaster buttons
i cut red chevrons
into my breasts
i tangle branches in my hair

i live like the goddess
the goddess of the sickle moon
and the straight rain
i am she who is a snake
i am she who is a crane

i am she who sees the glint
of a fish in the river
i am she who eats pig
and weaves wheat
into babies who suck deep

i am she who looks long
long into the water
i am she who sees the masks
floating and lonely and empty
i am she who has one eye

the fifth month

The womb hums
Alive with a thousand bees

That flap and turn violently
As a black and yellow butterfly

Trapped
By an amateur's net

The midwife says my uterus is
Stretched high between my breasts

An invisible thorax
Impaling my blue-veined and useless

Wings
White as the promise of lactation

She pokes and measures
Mutters a number in centimeters

But I cannot translate
I think only in fluttering circles

She advises more vitamins
Prescriptions in the alphabet of

Nutrition and guilt
Outside her pastel office

I crumple her piece of paper
Feed it to the zinnias

She doesn't know my baby's breath
Makes its own bouquet of honey

Or that I'm not ready
To nurture and mother

This queen of a creature
Already preparing to fly

Out of my randomly plotted garden
Out of my hive

Protected
Only by its stripes of powdery fur

the consort

I

all romance is a parody of this:
child
& woman as Madonna/Goddess

the day you learned to kiss:
the souring smell of my breast
on your excited wet breath

your giggles like the bluest baubles
on a sapphire necklace

more precious than precious

2

when i was engaged
i stole my mother's pearls
& hocked them
to pay for an abortion
for my lover's lover

then i eloped
alone
with you in my womb

& we gave birth
alone
in a room at the Desert Inn

3

that winter night
the stars brightly gossiping
& the moon
a bastard itself
almost full & approving

the cord was cut
by a paring knife
no doctor stitched me shut

there are scars
not meant
to be completely healed

4

no one needs to tell me
this is forbidden
:in bed together
sleeping through night after
cold night after hot night

our scent is so mingled
no animal could distinguish
between us

or would need to

5

i know how
Mary believed herself a virgin
never have i been purer
less subjugated
more sensuous
sweet sweet Jesus

something bares its rubied teeth
& howls
in the desert

the freeing of the hands

1.

women once walked on their hands
like dogs
like men
balance was easier
but it was difficult to get the babies
to suck
so they used their forearms
to scoop up their human pups
thinking that this might be freedom
standing up

but the men followed them
like dogs

2.

my five year old hand
sweating in his hand that was bigger
than a kitten
i asked: do you think
my hands will ever be as big as yours?
he laughed: i hope not

but there have been many times
i've wished my hands were as large
as cats
larger than my father's
gangs that could invade tough alleys
and thrive

3.

thirty seven stitches in my hand
the pinkie severed
the slip
of a knife   playing
chicken   playing   do you love me?
do you trust me?   no longer playing
take me to the hospital
call my father
who says: it will have to be amputated

but the woman doctor saves my finger
with prayer & catgut & gauze
when everyone asks me later
what happened?
i stand up
& convincing as a rooster at dawn
i lie

4.

my cousin's hands
shadows   of birds
wings   backlit by a nightlight
flying across a wall
landing on my body
my childish skin stroked like white
feathers   until the pink showed
through my shame

but not even my father noticed
my hands red as chicken necks
cut & bleeding
from trying to bend
the cage wires of my cousin's fingers
back   apart

· 5.

one day i decided to love my hands
as if they were cats
demanding incessant attention
but requiring only freedom

that night my father lost four
of his fingers in an extruder
his right hand pressed flat
as a hounds ear

i pick him up from the factory floor
pull his bloody weight
up to my chest
push him against my breasts

scream at the men who watch
while the rescue sirens howl
in the distance
like dogs

totem pole

I.

art has never been my talent
i cringed at every assignment
in the ninth grade graphics class
maybe i should have stayed in home ec.
she passed me the exacto knife, smiling

we were impressed with our status
as the only two girls in the room
i was reeling with some sacred knowledge
that inhaling her touch made me dizzy
like sharing a forbidden cigarette

the dull blade scratched me
lightly, like a baby bird landing
my world went storm dark
her arm flew to the sky
she asked for the hall pass

her voice echoed
persuading, insistent
she called her own name
inside my wooden head
the blade scratched deeper

into the pulp of my hand
when she returned i was beginning to bleed
she screamed, her mouth full of feathers
i was suspended
to commemorate the event

the design that stood carved in my flesh
was her name & i've always been grateful
for its brevity
its healed abstract quality
it could be any almost-lover, smiling

2.

it's like tapping for sap
only amateurs believe the needle
is intended to push anything in
the rest of us know its purpose
is to entice something out

the red cedar blood
ricochets through the syringe
like howling across the mountains
the days and nights are shadowed with silver
the incessant search against hunger

the veins splinter
the skin cracks
rubbed raw against the blue grain
track marks scar gradually
revealing a fierce canine face

burst blood vessels clot into eyes
the abscesses grin with pus-long teeth
this god-beast rests serene below the elbow
demanding no devotions, no sacrifices
its existence is sufficient religion

3.

i envisioned a fish
aqua and gently finned
instead it had black incisors
gripping another fish
gripping another fish

the tattoo swam across my forearm
the muscle gradually atrophied
underneath the little blades of ink
tearing into the mask of a lover
wearing the mask of a sailor

4.

the shoulder socket
a spruce root basket
frayed from daily use
the underarm a forest
a protected inlet

in the night i cradle her ocean
against the lonely winds
the paint on the walls is silent
the moon watches intently
through a window as i kiss her

5.

art has always been our talent
narrative can look ugly
my arm is more than the story
of our endangered tribe

we know a bird by its beak
a fish by her teeth
the wolf by its shadow
the moon by its bold eye

each lover wants to know
how i lost
those three fingers
        index   middle   ring

absent as the possibility
of a silver band
her name etched inside
or at least her initials

there is nothing to do except laugh
during the potlatch
this is when we exchange everything
we pretend we own

and each lover relearns
the making of love
two remaining fingers spread the horizon
wide wings of the raven

salt pink as a salmon
tracks from a pack of wolves
the moon is an animal
all the rest is myth

Part Two

*every self portrait
has been someone else*

White and Black Photography

The man at Ashmore's always asks me
whether I'm White or Black. I never answer.
I'm here only to buy my mother's dream book.
If you dream of Indians, the number 42.
If you dream of death, the number 9.
When my mother wins the lottery, she will buy
herself that fine white house on the corner;
the one with the triple windows and black shutters
that open and close. The neighbors will joke
about my professional quality tripod, calling it an old woman
with a cane or a young man with a hard-on.
I will laugh, ready to travel and photograph
across each of seven dark continents.

Elizabeth "Tex" Williams
Black Photographer
1924–

I married the military at twenty
and never divorced.   I shot
thousands — millions — of soldiers,
finally learning the right lightings,
the right timings, to prevent overexposure
of even the most ghost-like faces. I
preserved forever the soon-to-be-dead.

My first lover said I was gray in bed.
My second lover said I was dangerously unfocused
I pretended both times not to know what was meant.

My first lover had long white hair.
My second lover had a bald black head.
They were married, to each other.

They gave me their Japanese camera.
It was a present; they hardly ever used it.
If it was payment, I still would have taken it.

The first photograph I took was myself:
I was a shadow, the camera was a flash
that burned a white hole in the mirror
where my face would have been.

Berenice Abbott
White Photographer
1898–

Every age is dangerous for a woman:
the Age of Science, the Age of Reason,
the age of 23 when I escaped to Paris
to sculpt, but found strength instead
in the sharp subjects of women. Black
and white always; color only crowds
a photograph, like a man in an artist's life.

I want to marry a photograph
of my mother when she was my age. Her white
collar is starched skyward, like a supplicant
to some unnamed goddess of toughness.
I want to go to school, to the city, to somewhere
where I can preserve the sleek survivals
of women on high contrast paper.
I want to be a photographer.
But once among the gray buildings, I find success
on the wrong side of the mirror. I am a model:
the exotic, the object, the lie instead of the liar.
My mother sends back the money I send her, hissing
"slut." I purchase expensive new equipment.

Dora Miller
Black Photographer
1918–1951

Even my mother was excited by the scholarship,
impressed by the lettering on the vellum envelope:
The California Institute of Photography.
Nothing is free. I had to model, to answer phones
in the damned charm school. Still, I learned enough
to open my own studio in L.A., but not enough
to avoid a hard marriage, an early heart attack.

Like a marriage bed with running water,
like a passionate lover who is always at home,
my darkroom comforts. Pity my life
does not possess a safelight and a triple
goddess of plastic trays and
neatly labeled bottles of fixer
eager to stabilize every negative.
I want the ability to crop and dodge
my days, to increase the exposure time
of my stop-bath nights. My only weather
would be cool tones or warm ones.
I would choose my contrasts:
a whiter white, a bluer black.

Billie Louise Barbour Davis
Black Photographer
1906–1955

Before I was married I danced, but
now I leap in the laundry room. I lined
the windows with blackout shades from the War.
It was easy to do, almost as easy as shooting
the Virginia skies, cloudless with drought.
I huddle inside, manipulate the light,
execute prints which are exotically crisp.

It is my aunt who calls her whore-niece back
to the Florida hospital where my mother's body
bruises the over-bleached sheets. The White doctor
informs me there are 63 tests for the head.
The technician administers the EEG, explaining
it is like "little pictures of the brain,"
as she pastes pieces of cotton into my mother's hair.
Although the tiny cameras are held by my mother,
she is not the photographer,
but a photograph labeled "Pickaninny, 1935, Mississippi."
The technician switches on the strobe.
My mother is overexposed.
White light flashes where her brain should be.

Margaret Bourke-White
White Photographer
1904–1971

Black and white is the technique of reality.
I learned this in the thirties
as I photographed the Black Florida
sharecroppers, against their newspaper wallpaper, for
the book I was doing with my soon-to-be-second husband.
Later, they would say I lacked subtlety.
Later, they would send me to South Africa for LIFE.

It is a small exhibit of huge photographs, my first.
There is a polite white wine with a California label.
My lover of the moment has refused to come,
protesting that my work is too dark, as in "depressing."
My mother is a thousand miles elsewhere, dying.
My favorite print is 20 by 24 inches, with successfully
imperceptible graininess. Three Seminole daughters,
posed on the Everglades Reservation, in front of their mother's
government home. There is a triple window with black shutters
to their right, as partially focused as a childhood dream,
a sharp triangle of roof overhead.
No one buys this photograph.
Or any other.

Laura Gilpin
White Photographer
1891–1979

I wanted to know the Navajo I photographed
almost as well as I knew my Betsey, my
"companion of fifty years" as her newspaper obituary
labeled her. I never burned in the background sky,
cloudless or otherwise. I always waited
in the desert for the right weather. I never
wanted to work for LIFE, *only to live.*

I was a girl here, in this thin white house facing
the cemetery where my mother is being buried.
I learned my first shapes by tracing the headstones,
etched with names because of white powders or black metals
or lack of love. I learned life
was an image to be captured: transitory, tenuous.
I learned death was transparent. I vowed to be unmarried.
Today, I sit in the single window photographing
my mother's mourners: White, Black, and my own
grainy shade of gray. I cannot read the light
meter. Every exposure is wrong. When I develop,
I will burn in the faces, burn in a background.

Käthe Kollwitz, Graphic Artist, Sketches
A German Working-Class Woman

the distance between us is a piece of bread,
black and thick crusted. we both stand
on long lines, but i can pay you to stand
naked in my studio, pay you to stand
holding a child that is not yours. his
head is a pea in the giant pod of your hands.
i linger with charcoal, studying
the bulk of your fingers. i want
to etch each one with such concentration
that you will be mistaken
for a lithograph. i've always loved
hands. i've always loved
the hands of women. i've always loved
women. these are the reasons i married
a physician. and why did you marry
a worker in tortoise shell? and why
does he drink? i want to make you
beautiful. most of my subjects
are mothers and children of the fatherland.
do you believe i am asked why my art
is so tragic? but i want to make you
different. i have dreams
of week old babies. i have dreams
of you as a delicate hoofed animal
dancing in a forest. i have dreams

of innocence. i want to make you
a curve commanding space, a creature
that does not need to eat. wait,
why does your face twist as if you're
insulted? please understand, i'm weary
of my woodcuts of poverty, of struggle,
of hunger. another life, i would
have devoted myself solely to my hands,
sculpting the sweet earth into vessels.
but the death of children and women
demands sharper instruments. come, hold
me in your huge hands like you hold
that borrowed infant. wait, let me hold
you like a tree in the dead dead winter
can hold both roots and sky.

Regine's Rebuke to Kierkegaard

The years
flew by like magpies trailing bright
ribbons through the twilight. I
have fourteen sons. Not even one is
named Søren. Their eyelashes curl
dark and thick as the tails of Danish ducks
in winter. Some of my boys have handsome
fathers. Do not worry, my jejune darling, you
are not being charged with paternity.

The nights
I seduced you under my red coverlets
produced nothing; only your extravagant
guilt about acquiring a few basic skills.
It was distressingly easy to feign innocence.
The blood was a chicken's. I would blow
out the flickering romance of the candle and laugh
at you under my breath. Afterwards,
you would beseech God with your boring sins.

The morning
you decided you were too god-like to marry,
we sat on a hill round as my breast. The park
was fertile with spring and made me think
of all the places you had never kissed.
At that moment, you were more serious, more

tormented, more interestingly blond, than anyone
I ever knew, but your words were dishonest as parrots
caged as pets. I stilled the wings of my banter.

                    The day
you first touched me, you had taken me to
a museum in the city. One of us was explaining
the paintings of dead men, while the other choked
on the stale air. The halls were narrow as children's
coffins. As your fingers traced the braid round
the nape of my neck, I lifted my skirt to avoid
the curse of lust in a public place. Even then,
you did not guess I wore the feathers of a gypsy.

                    The future
you envisioned for me was bleak, but less
so than yours. Without crystal or leaves,
you foresaw my fatal flaw: the capacity to be happy.
You wasted your wind berating me. You
were fearful and trembling and sicker than death.

                    Your tragedy
was that you deflected your agony with eloquent
edifices, built to explain why you gave me up
when I was never yours to give.
                    My tragedy
was that your buildings were so expertly
mirrored, my messages died on carrier pigeons
crashing into images of boundless sky.

Mary Cassatt, After Destroying the Letters of Edgar Degas

I didn't burn them and they weren't about love.
You can think what you want. I want
you to. Imagination is a caress. Imagine

my portrait of him. I destroyed that too.
Not because he was the only man I ever
painted, except for my father and brothers,

but because I was giving up men
as subjects. I could never get them to touch
without blurring. His dancers weren't like women

I've known. He refused to connect them, to let
them look at each other. He called it control.
Even his whores were solitary, madonnas

out making a living while someone else
cuddled their children. I am interested
in something different. I love colors

like goddesses. Each one must be honored
and a place set for her at the christening
of each canvas, even if she chooses

not to attend; especially then. I love form
like the shifting earth: its lap, its curves,
its familiar kiss. He wrote about my body

calling it maternal, ultimately feminine.
He wrote that my works were substitutes
for the babies I deserved to have. He lacked

imagination. I never craved motherhood, virgin
or otherwise. I always imagined myself
as the infant in my pictures, the girl-christ, the

cherub. When there was no child but a lone
woman at her desk, I imagined myself
as the beloved letter for which she licked

the ugly tasting envelope. The answer,
in a masculine slant of unjoined figures,
had words so bland they tore themselves

to shreds in boredom. Imagine
that. No flames. No passion. Only
the drypoint of a newborn's cry.

The Animus of Diane Arbus, the Photographer

I've always been afraid of everything
Human. I was schooled in rooms with
Heavy drapes and taught that civilization
Insisted I ignore my cousin's prominent
Harelip. But I secretly studied it for
Hours, and learned that being polite
Is the ultimate savagery. I made collages
Of orifices that refused to be perfectly
Round. It was easy to let my eyes do
All my thinking; easier still to
Hide behind the three cameras I began to
Wear like gaudy necklaces. My goal was to make
Emotion one-dimensional. I photographed
What other people called freaks, but these
Were people I entertained, men and women
Worth at least one afternoon of dangerous
Sex. I wanted to develop the fear
Of the flesh. But I never thought
Anything was ugly—or beautiful—
Only that experience which teetered on the
Edge of consciousness seemed the most
Authentic. There is a thin lip
Around even the most gentle abyss
Of the soul. I circled and slid toward
Suicide, because all else is
Ambiguity, the cruelest focus of all.

Edith Lewis Comforts Willa Cather
as They Spend a Night
Lost in the Mesa Verde Canyons of Colorado

We are not lost. As a child, I was
lost often, by which I meant separated
from my mother. She dropped my hand to wander
in the dry goods store, where majestic bolts
of fabric loomed as high as pastel cliffs,
blocking the sun of the one I loved;
the one who did not love me, enough.

In this stone womb, twilight is as long as birth.
The moon rises yellow and round
with my vow: I will love you for the rest
of our lives, even if we survive
this night; even if we survive the next forty years.
You will forget Isabelle, forget Louise.
You will love me enough.

You will write of tonight on the mesa:
it was possession.
And yes, we are possessed, unborn, children
as pure as the silver whispers in the sky.
We can never be lost if we are together.
We are love. The world is our store.
Take my hand. Kiss the silence.

Another Version of *The Autobiography of Alice B. Toklas*

before her:
my voice is slit in two; the whispering
girl at home, silent almost / the whispering
woman who is answered by another whispering woman.
the question is California. there are only men
left in my family. and even the lesbians
are getting married. i learn to speak of Paris.

during her:
my voice is one half of two voices
fused as one. it is not only that we
can imitate each other perfectly
with the practice of years, decades, of hearing
one another hiking on that path
from outer ear to inner,
incessant repetition,
making it hard to remember what comes from outside
and what does not.
no, it is not only that.
it is that we have only one voice; one voice in the plural.

after her:
my voice is many voices. an echo.
low and raspy. knives thrown against canyons
with the lonely scrape of metal on stone.
grief did not silence me because i had to speak
for her.
but never for the one i would have been without.

Isadora Duncan Swims in the Sea at Sunrise
A Month After Her Children Drowned in the Seine

i first danced on the stage of my mother's water
safe inside her womb, like an oyster in a shell
shucked into the poor seaport of San Francisco
i believed myself blessed by the star of Aphrodite

even my bones hummed with the rhythms of water
i was afraid only of fire   my earliest memory:
the flames and my mother's screams for her sons
the police and their hoses swollen with water

now i want all memories to evaporate like desert water
as i search for the pink moon of Corfu, rising in the water
here in Albania children who are not mine are starving
their stomachs distended from gulping salt water

i open my eyes under the Adriatic's blue water
but see only blonde curls straight and dark with water
see only small bodies plumped like balloons filled with water
see only their chests, unmoved by breath, silenced by water

i cannot cry: that's how much i hate water
my tears would be dirty Paris river water
i am a goddess betrayed by my mother water
i wish this whole world would be flooded with fire

Romaine Brooks Names Herself Lapidé

In English, there is a distinction
between rock
and stone. I've forgotten it.
I lost my native tongue
in the mouth of a Parisienne woman;

in the mouths of many Parisienne women.
I decorated their expensive apartments
with the safe colors of caves.
I painted their interior portraits
with mute explosions of gray.

I had learned silence in the pits
of my mother:
an heiress of Pennsylvania mines,
a daughter of anthracite,
a wraith who will still inhabit

my drawings and dreams
half a century after her death.
My lover's cheeks grow bold in color
as she asks me this question:
how can I truly love women

when I was my mother's quarry?
I lick her lips and take
her tongue. I tell her I am
lapidé: my nickname for myself.
Her kisses are French.

My breasts are softly lonely.
Her fingers are Italy.
My spine is an arc.
I am softer than Venus,
but she says she's afraid

the statue of my body will crumble
from the earthquake of her passion.
I reassure my lover in English:
a rock
is much harder than a stone.

Self-Portrait of Frida Kahlo
Without a Moustache

I am land: Mexico. My leg
withered from polio dangles from my hip
like my country hangs off the continent.
My body is an unnatural disaster. My flesh
has been severed, sucked, impaled, and pierced
by machines, doctors, and men. Sometimes
my narrow back collapses as I paint. Sometimes
I wish I were like my husband, Diego
Rivera, as fat and as famous as America.
I adore him almost as much as I cherish
being unfaithful. I love making love
with women as elegant as Nicaragua, as
mysterious as France, as exciting as Nigeria.
Everyone I've ever embraced has been a substitute
for myself.

I am mortal: a woman. My eyebrows
grow together like broken wings. I dress
like a princess from the isthmus of Tehuantepec.
Rings circle every one of my fingers and a hand
shaped by Picasso bounces against my neck.
I eat sweet candy skeletons and have abortions
because my imagination is more elastic

than my abdomen. I like to make love
with huge wet leaves and drink *pulque*.
I receive close instructions from plaster
body casts which I decorate. I learn pure
pain is neither romantic nor endearing, though
my deliberate strokes can turn it tangible.
I spend the long silences of agony giving birth
to myself.

I am art: a creator. My palette
pulses like an Aztec heart torn from a still
twitching maiden. Sitting in an insanely
yellow chair, I don a huge man's suit and crop
my hair. I paint the words of a sad song over
this scene, on a small metal sheet, a *retablo*
without a saint. I keep pet monkeys, those Mayan
symbols of promiscuity. I tie them to me
with ribbons red as healthy veins. Our faces
wear the same expressions. I suckle from my
nurse's breast, her face a mask. I render my throat
laced with thorns, my self as doubled, my
third eye swollen with death or my husband.
Every self-portrait I've done has been
someone else.

Part Three

living my life as if—

Witchcraft in the Nuclear Age: thirteen accounts

1.

a cross-legged someone watches a red moon grow smaller
as it rises in Texas
all lights and eyes reflect the heat
the dogs, the cats, the pigs are silent
as they queue. flat and distant
a white bird glides to the left
like a heart, a bent feather, a witch's breast
the legs are uncrossed the eyes are cleared
the *wilde jadge* will end at the fences
spirits cannot be arrested
gather together again and again
some circles must be broken

2.

they stole our holy places, our holy days
once there was a sacred tree in this desert
the tree is long dead
the desert is in danger
they named the second Sunday in May for mothers
even as they said we would eat our own children
rather than tolerate their vapid warnings
we decided to worship their day
we gathered ourselves in Nevada
at a place they called a test site
we chanted in the searing daylight
the journalists wrote that all the protesters were women
the photographers discovered all the negatives were white

3.

the trials often start with charges of trespass
there is paper and handcuffs
and sons who replaced suckling
with the crease of a uniform
the ground is held as the most private of properties

by neatly guarded but public utilities
in the courtrooms, there are more guards
some of them are women
none of them smile in the fluorescent noon
there are books thick with rules
and numbers and penalties
the accused all state they have no names

4.

listen to the silos hum so close to the ocean
there is not enough salt in the world
to make heavy water float
children fall in love with this green
so iridescent it pales a cat's eyes
the toddlers want to touch this water
to swim, to drink, to splash
we are the women who restrain them
as we point to the turtles
with the red and swollen underbellies
rocking in the tides
we are the women learning invisible fire
we tell the children that water can burn

5.

all the roads spiral
around those long and low buildings
which squat on the shores of the Potomac River
a feather falls from nowhere
it is bent and as sturdy as an eyelash
you clutch it and massage it
into a lover's sweaty bed tonight
you draw pentacles on the Pentagon
you refuse to fondle the phallic Monument
every small protest is a necessary charm
against the promise
that you will be among the first to die

6.

for thirteen years, i curled around her feet;
her familiar, her dog, her protection:
a cop stalked her in Miami
my bicuspid tore at his tenderest flesh
a burglar busted our window in New York
my bark cut his hand on the jagged glass
we traded stories on winter nights
we swapped souls when it thundered
we travelled to Haiti together
she wove me a rope of herbs and hemp
we watched as the underbellies of clouds
turned green as turtles
we breast-stroked into the boiling Caribbean

7.

when i was a boy, i wandered the cities
San Francisco, Paris, Buenos Aires and Shang-Hai
i took older lovers from every country
i gave cures with potions of petroleum
i told their fortunes with round cards
men admired their hands on the curve of my back
so they paid for me to fly
everything was stopped by the blizzard of bombs
some men died immediately
some men died of disease
i like to think of each of them
i light red candles in their honor
using my fingers for flames

8.

there is ample anecdotal evidence for the belief
that witchcraft
co-existed with nuclear technology
and its aftermath
most of the official documents were destroyed, of course
but some stories survive even fire
this account is typical: a proud hag, somewhat
insulated by education, was working as a scribe
in a power plant when a man put his mouth
to her left breast and his hand over her mouth
she screamed and bit him and left a scar
he was something called a boss
she prosecuted him and she was found guilty

9.

we scratch beyond all borders
she & i
i wear 17 earrings in my African ear
all are melted silver
she has a braid from the left side of her head
it is singed blonde
feminus cum femina
i have the mark of the crescent moon
on my toe
she has a scar like a wild hare
on her back
we are each other after survival
she & i

10.

even at noon, the forest is dark
a green brown net
spun thin as glass
if i could find a window
i would hurry to the other side of it
i would look out it
i would pass through it
i would find the moon
i know she is still there
i know the wind is somewhere
if i could smell the tides
they would pull my heart
back to the left side of my chest

11.

if it's true that the devil's cock is cold
and always hard
like some steel building from memory
then let that bastard come to me
and fuck me and fuck me
i've been a lesbian since before i was born
but life is now too damned hot for us
i'm tired of women so soft
that when i stroke
their precious breasts
their raucous asses
their flesh rolls off
in layers too flayed to scab

12.

our ancestors met in caves
we must live underground
every place else it is summer
without a sun
our ancestors chanted at crossroads
we must sit silent
all other places are winter
without provisions
we are hibernation
we are meditation
i have shrouded my embryo
until she can grow
until i remember how to bleed

13.

in that last circle where all colors cavort together
and we have only enough strength to want
what is forbidden,
we dance
we dance   not with each other, and
       not for each other, and
       not with movements we will name
this is not the *danse macabre*
but even if it were, there is no one
left to persecute us
this is the dance of what we have always known
this is the color of what we tried to tell you:
the limits of all power are limitless

waves, night

the moon looks full, but it's waning
your mother
wails that she's tired   of life
at this edge   her same complaints
salted   over years
irregular as tides   out &
farther out   you are bloated
& have abandoned your attempts
to rescue her   or any other woman
including yourself

2.

we make our own traps, certainly
but what did you expect?   you were born
with the moon in cancer   born under
a steel pier   your first toys
were the sharp   & pliable wires
of crabtraps   you artfully constructed
your own prison   silly now
to say what you intended: *i thought
i was building a barricade   a home*

3.

Georgia O'Keeffe had no children
now she is famous
for Elizabeth Arden flowers   gigantic
in their femininity   famous also
for skulls & bones   of bleached white masks
raped from the desert   gleaming fertile
in unmitigated sun   not-so-famous
for her oiled testament   to her brief affair
with the midnight Atlantic   deep blue slants
& a pinpoint house of incandescence

4.

the not-yet-ripe peaches color
of shore light
five seconds before dusk   the suntan oil
color of beach foam   when there's a frantic storm
miles out at sea   the color you are tempted
to call yellow   the color of a single
fleck in the marine   blue iris
of your mother's   left eye
when she is angered   dangerous as broken coral
& as useless

5.

remember that woman writer, British
(something about a lighthouse)
(about a room)   the woman who walked
into a cold spring river   rock in her pocket
(something about death   being the only experience
she would never write about)   madness comes
not like a tidal wave   but like eddies
on a sandbar   the water is shallow & warm
harboring pieces of claws   & eggs frail as air bubbles
she had no children either

6.
your mother bays like a sea wolf
a mythical siren   a self-appointed
sisyphus   the waves crash her flesh
with dark rhythms   rimmed in foam
leaving patterns of white   like undecipherable runes
all round & content   salt renders choice
& fate indistinguishable   but the bait
is as shiny as ever   submerged in its slowly
too slowly   rusting cage of metal

a child's garden of verses

what i wanted was everything   in other people's gardens
twirling vines of purple flowers always in bloom
smells that spiraled from the grass   sophisticated
like cigarette smoke   gathering at my vinyl sandals
like the spring-pink braided garlands   in the library book on Heidi
like the double-heart ankle bracelets   adorning the whores on the corner
what i wanted was   a garden

a space   a sanctuary   a possibility
among the company of mountain-goat girls   and black-eyed women
feeding them   the vegetables of my labors   tomatoes
as huge as tires   red as the freshest stains on the sidewalk
potatoes   that grew salted and fried on towering stalks
i would cultivate corn   with rainbow-colored kernels   beans
that had seeds of butter   pumpkins with faces   round as babies

i would have fruit trees, too   cranberry sauce   blueberry pies
oranges that did not need to be peeled   nectarines   and cherries
with edible pits   there would be flowers, naturally
white blossoms   of all sizes   all breeds
buds folded, roses   swimming, water-lilies   tiny, soft as moss
i would bring home strays   like the striped-lilies
bent, exhausted   abandoned near the highways   dead by July

what i wanted was a fence   low enough to be hugged
far from barbed wire   no chains, no locks   what i wanted was a fence
wood, not metal   i would always keep it painted
bright inviting colors   like a trellis laced with morning glories
all day, every day   what i wanted was a fence
with a gate that opened   and shut
what i wanted was a garden   a verse from someone else's childhood

chain-links
(in three voices)

I.
She fell
under the spell of an older girl
drugs, dancing, and who-knows-what-else
together

She's fifteen and I've given her everything
she's ever wanted   I still keep her bottles
of juice   cool in the refrigerator   the nipples
clean   She's my baby   And I love her
I'm her mother   I have every right   to protect her

Just last summer   I called the State for assistance
They wouldn't give it   Only sent some social worker
who wore a soft silky blouse   and no bra
only a hot pink undershirt   underneath   as if she were a girl
Told me my daughter wasn't breaking any laws   by being wild

So, it's up to me to control   my daughter   flesh
of my flesh   bone   The streets could eat her alive
She doesn't know how to survive   Like I
did   I got the idea one night   from a TV special
the dangers of wolves   kept as pets
She never complained
when she was chained to the radiator
near her VCR and Chinese food
safe

When I heard about the girl   and the chain and the radiator
I almost forgot   I had been called by the mother
who showed me filthy baby bottles   as evidence of devotion
who wanted me to lock the kid up   throw away
her memory

When I investigated the case   talking to the neighbors
I wanted to forget   what they said
love   they told me   again and again   love
has to be tough   what do you know about drugs?
they challenged   about cruel lust?   about us?

they said yes   they'd seen the girl   chained day after night
she was happy   she had a VCR   Chinese food
she was   happy   They said sometimes
you have to hide them   hurt them   or even kill them
to get them girls   straight

When I talked to the girl   in foster care
I couldn't forget   myself twenty years ago
My mother screaming   she was going to kill me
kill herself   kill my girlfriend   I knew that girl
would go home

When I replayed the videotape   of my ex-lover on television
I tried to forget   to remember   the saltiness of her breasts
her voice was professional   she said these wolf-dogs
are wild animals   don't think feeding them from bottles
means they won't bite   don't think they can be trained

they'll never obey   they aren't as smart as they seem
they must always be chained   She accused me of infidelity
in the same modulated tone she used on TV   she knew all
about my half-moon romances   my pantings   like a bitch
in heat   i howled when she left me

3.

She bred me to be her best friend   bred me
for loyalty   to love her only   but she still wanted
my glint of wildness   a power only she could master

she taught me   to knit my own muzzle   to snap
my own leash   i won prizes
in obedience   i always came   before i was called

i never snarled   until i tasted escape
tongue on breast   sucking   biting
tasting the fur   of a whole new world

she tricked me   she trapped me   she chained me
to the glare of a TV movie   seen 28 times
to cold cartons of food   to her screams of betrayal

but rescue is no better   i smell their fear everywhere
it's as loud as the moon   they call it abuse
she calls it love   i call it

my choice   cunning   desire   my chance
my teeth   jutting around   a howling nipple
my howling nipples   my teeth bared   and hot hot pink

not for my mother & father

i'm sick to senility of childhood:
other people's & my own. i'm sick
in bed (with the flu) (it's
spring) & i'm reading (actually
leafing through) accumulated
literary magazines & journals.
every story & poem by a man
is about his father. or fishing
with his father. every piece
by a woman is about her father,
dying. nothing about fishing. nothing
about mother, who renders all art
sentimental at best, unless
the poet wishes her mother were dead.
has every writer been trapped
in the pains & pangs & fantasies
of childhood, still looking out
through the rusted grate of psychoanalysis
—that pornography for the cultured?
how sexy to see the small self (the
inner child) as victim, tortured. art
is determined at birth: to scrape
at explanations for adult idiosyncrasies
with the nib of a calligraphy pen.
as for me, i can't write because i had no
childhood. i was a woman always, caesareaned

at one hundred seventeen pounds
from a too thin slab of concrete; a
cracked sidewalk in east manhattan.
the doctor was a boy with a knife
& a four syllabled name, who taught me
how to fuck with a coke bottle. now
i know enough to call it rape (having
learned something from a talk show
psychologist) but then i thought i
should be silent & brave, as if i were being
born: with that much choice.
none of this is true, of course.
just a fevered delirium, but it's convenient
to believe autobiography
validates literature. i want nothing external.
really, i was born in the summer
to two parents who loved me, not
realizing they were too poor to possess
the capacity for love.
sad to say, none of that is true
either. i'm a practiced & obsessive liar,
having been born an orphan &
raised by the state (of Wisconsin)
(of Georgia), in a room pastel
as a warehouse. my bed had a pink
dust ruffle & boasted a silver
plate engraved with the number 117.
i still remember it. when i left,

when they turned me loose, i forgot
everything (like being born
at eighteen). forgot everything
except the number. except
the boy with the coke bottle
whose four syllabled name is now
in literary magazines, atop
blank verse about his father.
or fishing, alone in the city.

each winter

after the first chill sets   like a splinted bone
& my hands seem webbed   with paperish ice
you appear   blonde as my breath

i remember the months we lived   in our heatless
tenement   & you crossed each day off
the kitchen calendar   as if each midnight
were a splendid accomplishment

each dark morning   after the witching hour
we warmed our hands & cracked ribs
with sugared tea   lusting near the only window
for the sun   my arm in a sling

your eyebrows stitched slants   we pretended to read
a text on mythology   stared at each other
two battered Persephones   each waiting
for the other   to reveal herself

as Demeter   powerful mother who would rescue
us into a fruitful spring   by August
your patience had faded   you marked the book
at Antigone   & froze time into a private

eternity   the snap of your neck echoed
through the closets   the calendar
fell   from the unpainted wall
sweat chipped   at the ridges of your forehead

each winter
when i consider   my countless failures
first i count   the failure of my warmth
to thaw your flesh   my bones

ring the years   like pagan trees
documenting survival   as if endurance
of each cold season   since your death
                    were a brutal success

departure

loss is inarticulate   but not the drought that they say
instead it is wet   like tears and snot and
miscarried mucous   sliding through the vagina
like the stream   behind our backyard
that wants to be a river   (and some say it was
after that hurricane)   my nightmares flood the embankment

this morning's mail delivered   a catalog
advertising   a decorative redwood footbridge
fine-crafted in two sizes   weather resistant
easy assembly   for those who are good with a screwdriver
and a postcard   from the library
an apology: the book you requested is out of print

i am standing at the road   struggling to close
the metal mouth   of the moss-hinged mailbox
when i notice the rain   beginning again
and although   you have not been gone long
enough to accommodate   the most local of postmarks
such austerity stuns   no letter, no word from you

expectations are dangerous   they always said
(and you agreed)   i would be the one who leaves
the one who waits   for storms to cease
under the overpass   sheltered by concrete, while wiping dry
my motorcycle   contemplating only
the highway wide   silent, across the mesa

time, place, desire

the claustrophobic greens of late July
afternoons
as dark as dusk
last December, driving
across the nascent mountain ranges
plowed solid on the Cross Bronx Expressway
winter is an incessant memory
a song through the static of the car radio
the echoing voice of a woman
who just must be a dyke
winter is a frozen place
a formless knowledge
informing even the dawning of August

snow is a closet
cold as Colorado, that March, watching
her buying apples, lettuce seeds, an ax
i am innocent, visiting, i want
to tell her, i want
to ask her how she lives
in a state that hates her, i want her
she smiles like i just must be a dyke
nervous in Aspen, the ax
looks relaxed in her hand, shining like a silver necklace
after this last cup of latte together, i'm definitely catching
the bus, connecting in Denver
going home, toward summer, my lover

each season insinuates the others
every place breathes deep its comparisons
if i bury the bearded iris bulbs this autumn
they will bloom this spring
not as beautiful as California
but not as bald as those forced stems
in Provincetown, that white October
when she thought she just must be a dyke
but wasn't
by November
the rock garden frosted, i stayed until the season started
licking the shells of sea animals
souvenirs, repressed in the folds of my body

lust is a map and a calendar, i only want
to wander
and nest, simultaneously
i stuff my Swiss army knife into my knapsack and plant
shade-loving perennials, i polish
the chrome of my motorcycle and paper
the walls with designs for root cellars
my girlfriend says i'm schizophrenic
every Sunday
the librarian (she just must be a dyke)
inspects my selections:
A New England Gardener's Year
Handbook of Exotic Adventures

mint is frightening, it sprawls rudely in June
Hawaii is threatened by typhoons in September
i could infuse oil with basil and a hint of chives
i could visit Funafuti and dive the Dateline
straddle today and tomorrow like a native
but there is Monday morning, my job, its benefits
if you just must be a dyke, my first lover
advised: fall in love with your own survival
she did clip my nails, but not my desire
i still want
to be every woman
i ever wanted, even for a moment,
the one of us enduring everywhere

the ledge

you find yourself soaking in the sunlight meant
for the oversize bed of rock you stretch across,
from hard sharp pillow to footboard of plummet.

underneath you is the crevice, a labyrinth
of sheered formations. red arrows
mark the hand-holds for the scrambling hikers.

above you is the tower, a masonry square
with glassless windows. it boasts a view
of four states, which visitors enumerate.

you are waiting for your lovers to ascend
(or perhaps descend) and collect you,
you pose for strangers like part of the landscape.

the sun shifts in a direction you did not predict.
smoke drifts, but you cannot measure the distance,
every point looks half-way from the fuzzy horizon.

if you wait here long enough, the mountains
will set themselves on fire, sparked
by the fear of winter. you start to grow cold.

worry about your bones. how they carry codes
in their marrow. you count the flat-bottomed clouds
and the people you have known who killed themselves.

it occurs to you vaguely, you could throw
yourself overboard, to drown in the ocean of sky,
to become a mask on the face of the cliffs.

but you want to remain unpredictable. such
clichés belong in films about outlaws and women,
in nineteenth century novels, in nightmares.

you check your watch, again and again.
it seems you have spent most of your life waiting
for some purpose or some freedom to overtake you.

waiting for some person to fetch you,
some person who would never arrive because she was dead,
or you wished she was, instead of out flirting and drinking.

the rendezvous is unsuccessful. you shift to contingency.
which of your lovers was so paranoid, so precise,
to plan for plan B? of course, it was you.

you run down the trail, your back solid and stiff,
towards the place you separated, a gazebo on the lake.
they stare into space, hating you and each other.

"you're sunburnt," one pronounces, annoyed and accusing.
it would be better to have broken your leg, at this moment,
better to have dived into that broad delta, to have tried to fly.

it fades with the day. you trade stories, misunderstandings,
finally share anxieties, fantasies of danger and rescue.
picnic lunch has become dinner; its excellence earned.

by nightfall, all ruptures are invisible cracks.
life's rock-face is glacial: slow, smooth and majestic.
the flatlands have their own complications to master.

but on the moon shadowed ledge, your intaglio dances,
dressed in quartz and decorated with feathers,
closer to the crumbling rim than you ever ventured.

aesthetics

Beauty is a sunburn   midnight   heat-lightning
scars the sky   behind a stand of mis-matched trees
the irises bloom black as ink   the daylilies fist
of course, the moon flows full   invisible

summer solstice is a scratch   a masquerade
a stretch of sequins   stitched across the glowing bone
the elastic soaks blood   the plastic circles shimmer
my own hair   makes me shiver   cold   exposed

leaves in the shape of stars   of hands   of hearts
leaves in the shape of leaves   knives that tremble
tonight is a deep breath of green   an intermission
from the terrible arts of manipulation   the garden

every day she tells me she cannot continue   like this
the universe is ugly   and every evening i cultivate roses
ice-blue hybrids   prizewinners   frozen in a video
focused for sale   with music as advertisement

appearances   realities   analogies of caves
master the classics, they instructed   a needle in my thigh
i wrapped myself in myth   a gauzy gown of privilege
while she sewed lampshades   in a factory   night-shift

the wind is always, already   orange in the darkness
language is a kind of thunder   another art, education
but what is a text   without its translation?
there is no adequate preparation   for desire, threadbare

the last decade of patriarchy

1.

our old wounds got older
and less lonely   our fantasies fled our heads
to become schemes we swirled
like a dangerous coffee of safety

2.

a damp morning in any city
what a young woman sees is an old lady   sleeping
on the street   a random newspaper page
blows across the banged blue leg
the word *post-feminist* justifies its own column

heading other words
career   motherhood   having it all
the arrival of equality   reverse
discrimination   the wind still blows
the old woman could not read such words
even if her eyes were not swollen shut with cold

3.

there are conversations in restaurants:
"i no longer long to be chic;
even my boots are last year's color."
"i'm too old to be called a chick;
it wounds my fragile psyche."

the two women did not kiss then
but they would

they would think that kiss was enough
for a small revolution

they would learn how much more was required

4.

we don't want lifestyles
we want our lives

in this world, every woman is homeless

take back the night

reproductive rights for all women

all those words on our banners
in calligraphy, embroidery, blood and old stockings

we were marching
again and again and again
there was publicity
but it wasn't for us

5.

it had been ten years since i was married
but there were no anniversaries
no roses, no child support, no dinners
unless i made them

i was blue tired of the fumes of the factory
my mother died of cancer
no one to watch the kids during the day
at least at night they sometimes slept

you think prostitution isn't a solution?
all remedies are partial
in this god-forsaken world

6.

religiously, on sunday mornings
he fetches *The New York Times* and espresso
i pull out the magazine first
: another article on illiteracy
: an advertisement for effective resumes
: a photo-spread on Caribbean colors for livable living rooms

then we make love
he is gentle
i am not

i want to wound
i want to be lonelier than lonely

i have my fantasies: personal solutions
are political ones   no one
lives on the other side of my windows

7.

even with low heels and dressed in a dark blue success suit
she stumbles
again and again
on that same crumbled curb outside the mirrored building

the dimensions of her office are exactly
the same as those inhabited by men

on her desk is a pile of papers
she has learned to call documents
just as she has learned to call
her job a career
just as she has learned to speak English

to feel lucky
to forget the women walking the streets
          the woman sleeping on the street
          the wind swirling newspapers across her
          the blood crusting almost-blue

8.

we took back the night
every year for years

we reclaimed the moon
even after men had walked there

we had our rituals
we taught them to our children

we loved each other
and our love was a revolution
and our revolution was love

it wasn't enough
it was everything

we grew older and older
there are no words which can remember us

9.

you think to be unnamed
is to be safe?

you think buying coffee
from Nicaragua is brave?

You think your home
is comfortable?

You think there are no wounds
if you can't see them?

You think things are different
now?
yet?

10.

the Goddess, the Goddess, the goddesses
i've read my ninety-ninth book
on pre-patriarchal cultures
it's my last
i've memorized those slashes on their pots
(etched by women)
i've dreamed those womb-like hearths
(shaped by women)

there is still wind and there is still fire
the origins of inventions
no longer concern me

i am writing a book about post-patriarchal cultures
can you read it?

i am sipping a cup of mottled coffee
can you join me?

i am living my life as if—

will you?

Part Four

*the distance between
our love of masks
and our love*

text

I discovered her.

I invented her.

The first problem is not contradiction, but signification.

If the "I" is phallic—or even if it's not, it has been labelled such
and so carries the phallic connotation—then it must be confronted.

But how? There's the French slash: j/e, but attempts at translation
include the slashed I: I (too castrated, and thus too phallic)
and the italicized I: *I* (too slanted, and again too phallic).
I decide on the lowercase I: i.

It is not the lowercaseness of the "i" that makes me decide
it is disengaged from the phallic "I," but the dot:
that dot that can look like a slash or a slant or a direction or a point;
that dot that can look round and open as a you-know-what;
that dot that is so necessary it can be absent;
that dot that Cathi Kojinski drew as open hearts when she wrote her name;
wrote her name in blue ink on her school desk;
wrote her name in black ink in her school books;
wrote her name in purple ink on the hems of my dresses;
wrote her name in invisible ink on my thigh, just below my
curved red birthmark.

i discovered her.

i invented her.

Her who? Not Cathi Kojinski, but the "her" that kissed Cathi Kojinski;
the "her" that decided upon that lowercase "i" with its crown of possibility.

All identity is in question during these dangerous days of postmodernism.
It's risky to concede that "i" might be "her."

Risk is a noun. Risk is a verb.
All nouns must be mediated by verbs: to discover; to invent.
Verbs are demands.

The verb "discover" demands that "lesbian" be a noun.
The verb "invent" demands that "lesbian" be an adjective.

If i discovered her, then she is *a* lesbian, a noun uncovered in a pool
of essentialism.
If i invented her, then she is lesbian, an adjective constructed in a storm
of social forces.

i want her to be a lesbian, a noun, unmodified.

i want her to be lesbian, an adjective, free.

There is just no escaping grammar, which is what Miss K. tried to teach me.
Miss K. was a creative writing teaching, from Alberta, who hated
all things French. i did not have a crush on her, although her hair

was blonde and her eyebrows were black; very striking
on a white woman wearing red dresses as she did quite often.
Across one of my more interesting surrealisms (if slavishly derivative),
she scrawled: *Try to write something happy.*
She dotted her "i" with a perfect circle, replicated in the exclamation point
terminating her sentence. i wrote realisms of varied-colored women
with Cleopatra bangs and bloodied tracked arms. She wrote the same refrain
with the same open holes. i went to see her.
i told her i wrote what i knew. the sound of street. the smell of horse.
Pathetic, i said, wanting her to tell me it wasn't. She told me again to write
something happy. She told me to be imaginative. She said write fantasy.

   i did.

   She wrote: *please see me.*
There were no "i's" to dot.

   She told me not to worry. She told me it didn't necessarily *mean*
anything to have lesbian fantasies. To have lesbian fantasies is not to *be*
a lesbian.
"One need not base one's life on a few *feelings*," she reassured me. It didn't
mean much, she said, most probably nothing at all.

   Miss K. was a social constructionist.

   At least when it came to lesbians. In the presence of her
theory of lesbianism, i looked at my writing assignment and saw
something essential, immutable, incorrigible. i saw a lesbian.

There was no escaping this lesbian, which is what
i learned from Christine.
Christine lived across the street from me, in an apartment with her mother.
Christine was very cute, very Catholic, and very pregnant. After "little Philip"
(as he was always called) was born, Christine would stroll the baby down the
street. Sometimes "big Philip" (although he was smaller than Christine) would
walk with her. A few people thought i was interested in little
Philip, that like any young girl i wanted a baby of my very own.
No one thought i was interested in big Philip. Most people
thought i was interested in Christine; i was.
i thought she was romantic. i loved her insolent smile, her strange freedom,
her swollen breasts. And she walked like a dyke.

People gossiped that big Philip would not marry Christine,
but she told me different. She told me he had asked; she told
me she had refused. She told me she had slept with him because
her mother had accused her of "messing around" with some girl
named Mary at St. Catherine's parochial high school, from which
Christine would never graduate. She told me having a baby was
penance for her sinful nature; i guessed she meant Mary and not
big Philip. She told me she could not change, but that having a
baby would keep her busy.

At sixteen, Christine was an essentialist.

At least when it came to lesbians. In the presence of her
practice of lesbianism, i looked at my knees and saw something
shifting, challenging, changing. i saw a lesbian survivor.

i'm still contrary.

i like to think of Miss K. and Christine reading something
about lesbians in some essay by a writer named Nicole Brossard.
i like to think of Miss K. reading something
about lesbians blazing and reborn from essences.
i like to think of Christine reading something
about lesbians inventing everything because of their attraction.

But Miss K. got married and murdered, and would never read
a French Canadian even if she were still alive.

But Christine forgot everything she ever learned at St.
Catherine's, and reads only TV Guide.

And really, i don't like to imagine them reading at all.

i fled their lives; their constructions; their essences.

i fled to look for her; to work on her; the adjective verb; the lesbian lesbian.
i discovered her in a doorway, her face scratched.
i created her in the image of Kim Novak and Jack
Kerouac, who called himself a Canuck.

i think my story is happy.
i think my story is partial: fragmented into other stories, like the stories
of Miss K. and Christine.
And like all stories, such stories are false.
And like all stories, such stories are true.
And like all texts, this one is a tension
between fiction and theory.
And like some texts, this one rejects the contradictions
between discovery and invention.

But what about poetry?
What about the poem and the poet?

What about the lesbian lesbian:
constructed in her essentials;
essential in her constructions?

In her universality, i am unmediated by verbs, loved and lover,
imagined and remembered, vocabularized and deconstructed,
post-modernized and pre-historicized.

In her particularities, i taught creative writing once
(in a prison, perhaps to Miss. K's murderer); i became an unwed mother
(the records indicate marital status but not sexuality);
i completed the curve of my birthmark
into a permanent red heart
by a tattoo on my thigh;
high.

Nightshade

"Une lesbienne qui ne réinvente pas le monde est
une lesbienne en voie de disparition"
—Nicole Brossard, "Lesbiennes d'écriture"

I.

i am going away a little each day

i don't necessarily feel bad about this.
facts, my mother taught me, are facts.
nothing more.
but the other women i know, the women i call friends, the lesbians
i called family until i learned not to,
accuse me: "you lack imagination," they tell me.
sometimes they say it in French, a language beautiful
as a slap on a high cheekbone, reminding me
of all the things i could never do:
plié, tour jeté, arabesque,
order in a restaurant,
sound like i came from Manhattan instead of the Bronx.

i wonder what happens to clichés
in translation; things like "every woman is
a lesbian because she loved her mother first."
i've always liked that one.
i never asked my mother what she thought about it.
i was one of those kids who kept her mouth shut.

i never told my mother that i loved her.
we were women who believed there were places words could not go.
though i loved her most, i think, the day she let me quit the ballet
lessons i hated so much they made my throat sore as silence.

II.

i am going away a little each day.
i am not lonely, although i get a bit bored, divorced
from the gossip.
so i start to make up stories: amusing, witty, meaningful;
my family—i mean, community—doing delightfully raucous deeds.
i laugh. when Margot asks me what is so funny,
i tell her a story about Glenda&Sammy&Gloria and their three-way
romancing under the nightshade while the cat watched.
she doesn't laugh.
she brings back Glenda&Sammy&Gloria for a confrontation
of epic proportions. i tell the same story,
"to their faces," as they say, only
i change the cat to a snowy owl and make the nightshade a
bloodier purple.
no one laughs.
Margot shouts that i am a liar.
Sammy says i'm crazy.
Glenda&Gloria agree i need therapy, but i know
that even if i had the money to slink into someone's sliding scale,
i am unpatient-able.
i have slept with every therapist in the state,
or if not her, then her lover,
or if not her lover, then i would tell her i had.

III.

i am going away a little each day.
someone sends my ex-lover to fetch me as if i am an empty pail of water.
Jackie—or so she was called when she was my lover,
　　　though now she insists on Jacqueline—
has always wanted to be a writer. Jacqueline,
even when she was known as Jackie, has always said she is a writer.
once i told her that to be a writer, one had to write
something. that's when she kicked me out. after
a mediation session, of course.

when we were together, she'd read Brossard in bed, first
in French, then in English translation, then in French again.
she called us lov(h)ers. i liked that.
i thought there was a world, as original as the wheel, invented
in that "H" so snug in its parentheses.
i never told her that my mother did not know what parentheses were;
that my mother saw them on a sign once, and became scared, as if
there was yet another letter, another signal, she could neither read nor write.

i am one of those women who keeps her mouth shut, at least
about certain things. still, i thought that Jackie, if not Jacqueline,
might understand my stories. but these days
Jacqueline is re-re-reading Virginia Woolf and quoting
something about the sacrifice of truth being "abject treachery."
Jacqueline also tells me that a story isn't a story unless its written,
otherwise it's a lie. "what about oral history?"
i ask her. "history," she says, "is history. nothing more."
she's becoming as tight-lipped as the British.

i tell her i am going to take a trip.
i tell her i'm going somewhere, where i will get away
from both French and English. she buys me a calligraphy set
as a *bon voyage* present. she must think i'm going by boat.

IV.

i am going away a little more each day.
truth: Jackie/Jacqueline had said.
vérité: in French.
but it's the wrong path, no matter which fork
i choose. i am interested in something different, less boring.
a fact is nothing more
than a fact, as my mother always said: she was a woman who never put facts
in parentheses.

(but could i kill the trees to say something?) there was a paper in the kit
from Jackie; white as bladderwort, dead as timber.
i practiced Gothic lettering.
i changed the story: i told myself how my family
representative of patriarchy made me abandon the only thing i ever loved
because girls should not be seen in leotards. i practiced
the lie of my love for Mme. Claudé, my ballet teacher.
i liked that one. i would never ask my father what he thought.

it was easy to rearrange the world once i started.
first, i moved the Bronx into Manhattan, confined it all
in the East Village. my mother was an artiste, didn't you know?
she was a poet and a painter and a radical revolutionary who could bake cookies
and braid my hair and read Flaubert all at the same time.

i was a dancer (not in the topless clubs
which supported me and my lov(h)er (not Jackie, or even Jacqueline)
the junkie) in the Royal Ballet.
my lover was a gorgeous choreographer. we were both
very political and went around changing people's lives for the better.
we had seven cats, all named for characters of Colette.

V.
i am going away a little more each day.
farther & further
and no longer caring that i can never remember the difference
between those two words. (is there one?)
my writing is getting smaller & smaller, not only because i'm becoming
practiced in italics, but because i'm running out of paper.
the trees grow more alive each night.
living in the woods, romantic as the witch i've always wanted to be, but
without the vocabulary.
my mother never taught me the names of plants.
i call most things nightshade.
my mother taught me never to take food from strangers.
i name most things deadly.

i am hungry. i am thirsty as an empty pail of water. the days dance
shorter & shorter. in the winter sun, i recognize
rabbit bells (a memory from a walk with Margot
                                    her: spouting off botany
                    me: telling of Glenda&Sammy&Gloria).
the dried pods pop like children's guns.

the seeds are small and shiny, accurate as obsidian.
i wonder what would happen if i eat this jewelry?
if i don't?

or i could gather bunches of them, go
to a Women's Craft Fair, and market them as lesbian rattles.
i could write "grown on sacred lesbian land" in well-rounded
calligraphy on vellum notecards.
i could make my fortune.

VI.

i am going away a little more each day.
no one knows where i am, or everyone does, but no one cares, which is nearly
as good as being invisible.
if i can't be seen, i can't be shot.
i am one lesbian, living alone in the woods.
i am not one or the other of two lesbians, camping, when a crazed man
(as if all men aren't) (oh, father, forgive all words supported by parentheses)
aimed his rifle and fired&fired&fired&fired&fired.
both women are shot.
one can't move & the other can.
one goes for help & the other stays.
one dies & the other doesn't.

the one walking, the one trying to hold her blood on the right side of her flesh,
does she try to reinvent reality?
does she try to spin the world back to a safer moment:
when both women were walking & spotting a plant on the trail,

trying to identify nightshade?
does she feel like disappearing?
do her bones scream for her lov(h)er?
while back at the campsite, a woman, a lesbian, each breath
(like an "H" trapped in parentheses of blood) closer&
closer to the last one, closer&closer to that place
where words don't go.

> (at the man's trial,
> his defense is that his mother
> was a lesbian.)

VII.

i am going away a little each day.

i am one lesbian, disappearing in the woods, trying to imagine
that those two women made love/slept/broke camp/and
are now safely home arguing
with sharp words about how one of them told a lie (oh, so tiny)
to the other one. i am trying to imagine which one suggests
mediation. the dead one or the not-dead one.

i want to reinvent, not the wheel, but those two women.
i want to tell them that Jacqueline is Jackie
and that her tongue licks me instead of slicing me.
i want to tell them my mother read Bauldelaire.
i want to tell them i was born in Paris, *s'il vous plait.*

i want to tell them about translation: a French phrase
i cannot read, except for *lesbienne.*
one woman translates literally: who does not reinvent the world.
one woman translates differently: who does not reinvent the word.

i want to tell them that the hurricane that is coming is not
a hurricane, but a simple storm;
no, not even a storm, but a change in the weather;
not even a change, just something i will name: nightshade.

the winds of nightshade are strong.
the trees bend like parentheses.
the rains of nightshade are sharp.
the rabbit bells are pierced like spitting jewels.
this world—
this word—
i have not invented could kill me.
i must reinvent.
i must reinvent this roar which sounds like many men with many guns.
i must be a lesbian who will not disappear; unless it suits me;
i must be a woman who will speak only in my own language,
unless i find another.
i must be the girl who loved her mother first.
the boy who did. the boy who loved his mother, the lesbian.

my throat is smooth from screaming out "nightshade."

the world—
the word—
i have reinvented, spins beautiful as the first wheel making the wind gentle
as a mother's slap,
making the rain round as it fills the pail of water.
or so she wrote.

la lesbienne d'écriture.

historicity

This place—like all places—has a history.
There are mauve walls with paint blistering to reveal
penicillin-urine-yellow patches.
There is a reception area; there are conference rooms.
In storage, there are old files, minutes of meetings, annals,
calendars, appointment books.

This woman, with her four fingered hand and fuchsia cotton boots,
like all other women—whether or not their hands are missing
their pinkies; whether or not their boots are cloth—has a history.
As she walks through the front door, she brings her history with her.
Otherwise, she is alone.

It is time for the presentation.
Someone is going to lecture on "The History of the Program: How
We Got Where We Are and What It Can Tell Us About Where We Are Going."
The woman puts down her pencil. Everyone else picks up their pens.
She tries to decide whether or not to resign from this board of
directors, to relegate yet another political organization to the
resumé of her past.

Yet she believes women's organizations have meaning; that they
must have meaning.
She has said that just because we are historically constructed,
that doesn't mean we cannot construct our own histories.
She is weary.
But everywhere women are dying and this woman feels weariness is a privilege
to which she is not entitled.

There is the ritual coffee afterwards.

Later, and elsewhere, the woman walks
with another woman.
They walk deep into a state park which bounds a federal prison.
They walk down paths, through scrub, over railroad tracks. They
pass a fenced pasture:

> *I always thought those fields were natural.*
> *Miraculous. It hurt me, as a child to figure*
> *out that people had chopped down*
> *that forest and cleared the land.*
>
> *I wonder if it hurt the land.*
>
> *I think so, but it was a long long time ago.*
>
> *We become used to the pain.*

They walk to the lake.
It is empty of water, except in the deepest middle,
except in pockets indented like the flesh of thighs giving way
to a caress.
There has not been much rain of late.
They walk through the basin.
Grasses that once floated or fed fish now swirl sun-dried brown
over similarly dried stalks.
They remind one woman of tepees on the Great Plains that
she has never seen.
They remind the other of burial huts south of the Sahara that
she has never seen.

The woman do not exchange their ideas, for they are still caught
in the experiences of their own lives; experiences which have
taught them that because all exchanges are uneven, they must
insure that every bargain is scrupulously fair.
And it doesn't seem fair to voice something which one has not
personally witnessed.

The two women walk farther.
A snake like a missing finger
slithers over one woman's foot, up her pants toward her ass.
She jumps, but does not scream.
The other woman brushes the harmless creature from the woman's leg.

Snakes make me nervous.

Forget Eve. Remember Ishtar, Oya',
beauty of Medusa, any goddess you choose.

It isn't that. No, it isn't the history
of the world. It's my own history.

When the woman stop walking, they stand still in the morning,
the sun over their shoulders, a waxing moon in the corner, over
the pasture.
They begin to trade childhoods.
Images.
What they usually do not talk about.
They resist organizing the past as if it had led inexorably
to this moment;
but it is becoming more and more difficult.
They begin to tell each other of the other women in their lives;
of other lovers.

There is much that neither woman says:

> *Once a man told me that when two people*
> *begin to talk about their romantic affairs,*
> *it means that they are on the brink of one*
> *themselves. But I was shocked when he said that*
> *to me. He was much older than me and I had*
> *never been to bed with a man. Sure we'd*
> *been talking about my girlfriend and he'd*
> *been telling me about his wife, but I only*
> *had the need of conversation.*
> *No, this is different.*

> *Once a woman told me that we never get over*
> *our first lovers.*
> *Well, maybe that's true, but my first lover is*
> *dead and a corpse is hard to get over or to not get over.*
> *Sure, maybe I'm doomed to always be looking*
> *for a replacement; or equally doomed to*
> *become involved only with people who*
> *couldn't possibly replace her.*
> *No, this is different.*

But what they do say is more than either of them has said to
anyone in a very very long time; perhaps longer than either of
them has been human.

Each cannot believe the other—believe herself—is so revealing.
Each wants to use her opposable thumb to clasp the other's hand, hair.
Each remains standing side by side, speaking in stories:

I was in graduate school, trying to learn;
trying to learn to teach; trying to teach
the philosophy of history; trying to deconstruct
the theories of linear time; of progress; of individuals
as coextensive with ideologies. But that's not what
was popular. People wanted to know the history
of philosophy: which man thought what and when.

When I was in graduate school in literature, trying
to learn what other's had written and what was left
for me to say, one day I was sitting in my windowless
office with the door shut tight. I was not
smoking a cigarette, though I wanted one.
My hair blew across my face, becoming hooked
in a silver crescent-shaped earring. Those
strands remain there, even after I
chopped off my hair and sold it.

The women listen to each other's stories: attentively, passionately, seriously.
They listen with all the grace of a search for a missing object—
when the object is unknown.

Both women are college educated; post-graduate educated; degreed
and tenuously validated.
Both women are privileged beyond the historically constructed
conditions of their gender;
of their sexuality clinically classified as deviant;
one is privileged beyond the bounds of her class.

Their privilege is within the ambit of their shared light-skinned, blue-eyed, unmistakable whiteness; their shared nationality built on continuing histories of imperialism; their shared place in a post-industrial, post-feminist, post-technological time. The women are privileged to sit in meeting rooms with or without windows and listen; to stand in classrooms and talk; to take notes as well as to give them; to converse over coffee. Both of them feel strangely privileged not to be among the dead.

But nothing in their histories prepared them for each other. Or everything did.

The two privileged women hear a train.

One woman winces at the whistle. Trains remind her of the transportation of great numbers of people to their death. She is a young women, not yet born during World War Two, but as she turns to face the sun and the train, her vision is clouded by smoke from ovens burning the bodies of Jews, Gypsies, Gays and anyone else who somehow failed to be blonde enough, masculine enough, cruel enough.

Walking back, following the tracks, the other woman stumbles on a spike. She winces, not from the pain, but because each tie reminds her of each body conscripted to lay the tracks across America. The Chinese, the Blacks, the convicts, all the immigrants. And all the people who inhabited these lands and were wrongly called Indians and fought this snake that slithered with disease and liquor and guns. And the rails, extending into infinity like the limbs of prostitutes, stretching in

a country where it is less treasonous to trade sex for money
than it is to trade stories,
than it is not to trade.

> *Sometimes I wish I didn't know. Wish I*
> *hadn't read anything ever.*
>
> *Those who don't know history are condemned*
> *to repeat it.*
>
> *Who said that?*
>
> *Some man. Some time.*
>
> *I don't want to know the history of men. I*
> *don't believe in being condemned. I don't*
> *believe repetition is failure.*
>
> *I have to pee.*

This bedroom—like all rooms—has a history.
There is dusty rose wallpaper, with an abstract design
in white which could be a shell or could be a rose or could be neither:
it could be an abstract design which refuses to be anything other than itself.

These women, with their fingers moving across each other's faces
and their bare feet, like all women who dare to attempt love—whether or not
they have flinched when others touched their jawbones; whether or not
they have fucked men with shoes strapped tightly on their ankles—have a

history that is becoming shared.

The women are not alone.

In this room, the wallpaper only partially masks the slow ache of death.
The ones who accomplished some part of their dying in this room blistered
some parts of their living into the hollow plaster.

It is a strange place to make love,
but perhaps no stranger than any place else.
Still, it is strange to arch diagonally across the bed
which belonged to one woman's parents. She wasn't conceived on this
mattress (rather, in the brutal back of a Hudson), but her mother once
threw her down on this bed so hard that the pastel pink diaper pin unstuck from
her skin and she stopped screaming. She hasn't screamed since.
Even when she comes, she shoves one of her four fingers into her
mouth, as if silence were a solution.

Except now, something is different.
Without stopping to decide, one woman takes the other woman's hand
from her mouth and puts it in her own.
This is not a ritual.
They will drink coffee on the porch in the morning, letting the light
wash over them like a template of some prehistoric dawn.

Later, and elsewhere, after meetings missed to make love, after
conferences in which one woman could only think of the other, after programs
and articles and long distance telephone calls, after disentangling

histories shared with others,
the women walk
in a place they have been before.

Under their feet are artifacts: a condom, a Miller Lite bottle,
a rock sprayed fluorescent yellow, gum wrappers, a cardboard
tampax inserter slowly decomposing,
but the women do not look down.
They look at each other.
When they come to the fenced pasture, it is not empty. There is
a horse, huge among the calves. There are a couple of cows off
to the far side, nuzzling each other and then not nuzzling each other

Sometimes I feel we speak without talking.

I used to feel ridiculous holding hands.

They walk to the empty lake, which is soggy now in spots. It has rained.
There are birds this time. A solitary heron. A flock
without a discernable pattern.
The women find a dry spot.
They hand their jackets to each other, laughing, then sitting down.
They use their hands to shield each other's eyes from the sun.

My sunglasses are amber tinted and make
everything look jaundiced.

Like a hurricane.

Were you here for the hurricane?

No, I was somewhere else in a different
hurricane. I know a woman who was struck by
lightning, but it wasn't in a hurricane.
She walked back to her house afterwards, got
undressed and into bed next to her lover.
Then she died.

They want to take off their sunglasses without squinting. They want
to take off their clothes and let the sun be the only wall that surrounds them.
They want to make love.
But at this time in history, in the places these woman have been, women
do not do such things,
unless it is dark,
unless the land underneath them is "owned" by at least one of them,
unless they can forget certain historical facts—nine million
women burnt as witches,
unless they can pretend they have never know about certain dangers:
soldiers, hunters, policemen, guards of concentration camps and
prisons, men having fun.

Each women has a sentence about history which she thinks is both
too stupid and too intellectual to reveal:

> *We can only know a fragment of history. We*
> *know that it can never be enough, even while*
> *we know that it is much more than enough.*

> *History is the tale of survivors written*
> *with the pen of guilt in the bloody piss of*
> *the dead.*

The women spread their fingers toward each other instead and try
to free each other with scraps of language:

> *Once—or perhaps more than once—when I*
> *lived with a woman of adolescent beauty and*
> *politics, her brother came into our bedroom*
> *and raped me. He fucked me in the ass, over*
> *and over, while she watched, hugging her*
> *silence like a dead cat, pissing all over herself.*
> *I watched her and she watched me*
> *until we couldn't remember who was who*
> *except that neither one of us could ever be*
> *her brother.*
>
> *Sometimes when we talk about what we've done*
> *in bed with others, I want to puke. It's*
> *not that I've ever been sorry. It's not*
> *that I have regrets. It's only that I've*
> *had hundreds of other bodies and I now want*
> *my body to be as different as this is. I*
> *want to do things with you that are*
> *objectively—historically—distinct. But I*
> *suppose that's impossible.*

The women listen to each other, knowing their stories are more,
knowing their stories are less than attempts at historicity:
authenticity derived from historical fact.

Both of the women exist in this world.
Each act of each woman occurs within an historical context, but also
with-out it.
There are acts which are recorded and acts which remain
unrecorded and there is no difference in the reality of these acts;

in the clarity of these acts.
There is an act which their backs arch toward.
There is fear of reprisal.
There is something beyond fear; some belief that life can be
more than the opposite of death; that immortality has nothing to
do with being remembered; survival is not the ultimate goal.
The women take off each other's clothes.

> *I've always had theories, politics,*
> *philosophies.*

> *I've always thought desire was historically*
> *constructed.*

> *I've always wanted you.*

> *I want you now.*

There are places with histories and perhaps this will always be true.
There are rooms where people died, or people did not die,
or there was coffee, or there was sex traded for money or sex
that was rape. There are meetings and classrooms
and memories of graduate school.

But there is also this:
two women abandoned their histories
and the histories of every world they have ever known
and made love on the soggy ground of what is sometimes a lake.
No one came to kill them. No one came to embarrass them to death.

And after they had made love in ways they thought impossible,
they walked to a mound of dried grass and they spoke
of how it reminded them of historic rituals of death;
they urinated standing up and commented on each other's yellows
stark as the sun or soothing as the summer moon.

Everything led them to this moment.

And nothing did.

Everything leads them away from this moment.

And nothing does.

authenticity

there were other things that could have been said
about distance and love

i never escaped entirely
i learned withdrawal
i never denied my history
i edited it

this morning i watched men mow grass in the graveyard
across from city university
no matter how crowded or intelligent,
there is always room for death
i wanted the mist to cling like halos to the mowers
instead of shackles around their ankles
unlockable because untouchable
i wanted my lover to rise like an archangel
bearing a beautiful parking space,
crowned with a garland of brilliant footnotes

there are other things i could have said
about death and my lover

i have killed myself twice now
and am qualified to lecture on the vagaries of survival
i have loved her too long now
not to keep quiet about the nuances of passion

this summer, i'm the only one i know
who isn't in therapy or suing her therapist
who isn't recovering from her mother's death
or incest
i want to live on a beach in New Zealand
with a sheepdog smelling of kiwi
two hundred miles from a library
i want these days to be a flashback, backlit
by a beautiful blonde sun
bleached, burnt and hazy as a cherub's hair

there were things i heard them say
about her and the city

she was supposed to be a mirror, a knife
she is neither
here was supposed to be a culture, a life
it isn't even close

this year, i'm taking my lover and leaving the city
this place where only nature is unnatural
this place that makes me worship any pink inch of light
i am the mirror, the knife
with my dull side always out
shininess and sharpness are dangerous here
and never adequate as self-defense
i am the fence with garbage stuck in my throat
too frozen to decompose
or too styrofoam

there are other things i cannot say
like who i am and who i'm not

i thought fiction was poetry
it is theory
i thought theory was a solution
it is practice

this lifetime, my excuse is postmodernism
my identity is nothing other than a sin
called essentialism
authenticity is worse than co-dependency
it's self-dependency, how ugly
we were alone
trapped in a gridlock
when we lost
our sense of humor, sold
our imaginings of each other for tenure

there are other things we still need to say
about the streets, about the academy, about

the distances between our love
of death and our love
of masks and our love
for each other and our love

Notes

"neolithic": The conceptualization of paternity and the use of masks are described in The *Goddesses and Gods of Old Europe, 6500-3500 BC*, by Marija Gimbutas (Berkeley, California: University of California Press, 1982).

"white and black photography": The biographical information for Elizabeth "Tex" Williams, Dora Miller and Louise Barbour Davis is derived from *Viewfinders: Black Women Photographers* by Jeanne Moutoussamy-Ashe (New York: Dodd, Mead & Co. 1986). The biographical information for Berenice Abbott is derived from "A Life of Her Own," by Erla Zwinger in *American Photographer* 16:54-67 (April 1986). The biographical information for Margaret Bourke-White is from *Margaret Bourke-White* by Vicki Goldberg (New York: Addison-Wesley 1986). The biographical information for Laura Gilpin is from *Laura Gilpin: An Enduring Grace* by Martha A. Sandweiss (Forth Worth, Texas: Amon Carter Museum 1986).

"Käthe Kollwitz, Graphic Artist, Sketches a German Working Class Woman": The biographical information is derived from *Kathe Kollwitz: Women and Artist*, by Martha Kearns (New York: The Feminist Press, 1976).

"Self-Portrait of Frida Kahlo Without a Moustache": The biographical information is derived from *Frida: The Biography of Frida Kahlo*, by Hayden Herrera (New York: Harper & Row, 1983).

"The Animus of Diane Arbus, Photographer": The biographical information is derived from *Diane Arbus: A Biography*, by Patricia Bosworth (New York: Alfred A. Knopf 1984).

"chain-links": Some references in part 1 are to journalistic reports of a fifteen year old girl whose parents chained her to a radiator in their apartment. "Teen-Age Girl Found Chained in Bronx Residence," New York Times, at A35, September 15, 1991; "Girl Chained by Parents Says She Wants to Stay Home," New York Times, at B1, September 17, 1991; "Behind Girl's Chaining, the Call of the Streets," New York Times, at A1, September 20, 1991.

"text": The reference to Nicole Brossard is derived from the essay, "Kind Skin My Mind," in *The Aerial Letter*, trans. Marlene Wildeman (Toronto: The Women's Press 1988).

"nightshade": The selections and translations excerpted from *La lettre aérienne/ The Aerial Letter* by Nicole Brossard appear with the kind permission of Nicole Brossard from *La lettre aérienne*, Nicole Brossard, Les Editions du Remue-ménage, Montreal, 1985; translation by Marlene Wildeman, *The Aerial Letter* (Toronto: The Women's Press, 1988). Some references in Part VI are to the murder of Rebecca Wight and the attempted murder of Claudia Brenner by Stephen Roy Carr on the Appalachian Trail.

About the Author

Ruthann Robson is a professor at the City University of New York School of Law. She has been recognized by the *Village Voice* as the nation's "leading authority on lesbians and the law." She is the author of four books of fiction—mostly recently *Another Mother* and *A/K/A* published by St. Martin's Press—five books of nonfiction, and numerous articles of legal scholarship. Her poetry has been published in *Calyx, Conditions, The Madison Review, New Letters, Nimrod, Trivia, Kalliope, Florida Review, Common Lives/Lesbian Lives*, and in the anthologies *Early Ripening, Labour of Love*, and *Speaking For Ourselves: Women of the South*. She is the winner of the Ferro-Grumley award for Fiction, twice a Lambda Award Finalist, and a nominee for the PEN/Faulkner Award.